If you have a home computer with Internet access you may:

- request an item to be placed on hold.
- renew an item that is not overdue or on hold.
- view titles and due dates checked out on your card.
- view and/or pay your outstanding fines online (over $5).

To view your patron record from your home computer click on Patchogue-Medford Library's homepage: **www.pmlib.org**

IN THE ZONE

SKATEBOARDING

RENNAY CRAATS

Published by Weigl Publishers Inc.
350 5th Avenue, Suite 3304, PMB 6G
New York, NY 10118-0069

Website: www.weigl.com

Library of Congress Cataloging-in-Publication Data
Craats, Rennay.
 Skateboarding / Rennay Craats.
     p. cm. -- (In the Zone)
 Includes index.
 ISBN 978-1-60596-120-0 (hard cover : alk. paper) -- ISBN 978-1-60596-121-7 (soft cover : alk. paper)
 1. Skateboarding--Juvenile literature. I. Title.
 GV859.8.C73 2010
 796.22--dc22
                                    2009005599

Printed in China
1 2 3 4 5 6 7 8 9 13 12 11 10 09

Weigl acknowledges Getty Images as its primary image supplier for this title.

Illustrations
Kenzie Browne: page 7 Left.

Heather C. Hudak Project Coordinator
Terry Paulhus Design
Kenzie Browne Layout

CONTENTS

P eople have rolled on wheels for centuries. Early on, they roller skated or rode scooters. Later, adventurous people removed the handlebars from their scooters. This left them with a plank of wood on wheels—the skateboard. Skateboarding took off in California in the 1950s. A surfer named Bill Richards and his son, Mark, thought it would be fun to try surfing on land. Surfers and other athletes were thrilled with the new sport. It caught on across the country. Over the years, the equipment has been improved, and new tricks have been devised. Skateboarding is now a popular and exciting sport around the world.

Wooden scooters were early forms of skateboards.

Skateboarding is a sport of balance, skill, and courage. Some of the tricks can be scary at first—many skateboarders use ramps to help them soar and flip through the air. Skateboarders, or skaters, stand on the board and use their back foot to push them forward. They shift their weight from side to side to change directions. To stop, skateboarders sometimes flip the front of the board up and scrape the back on the ground. To prevent their boards from wearing out, skateboarders can slow themselves by dragging their back foot on the ground. There is no limit to what a skater can do. They ride down stairs, off benches and rails, around parks, and anywhere else they can think of to skate.

Sports History

Learn more about the history of skateboarding at www.kidzworld.com/ article/6543-great-moments-in- skateboarding-history.

Getting Ready to Skate

There is more to learning the sport than just stepping on a board and skating. Athletes need to make sure they are safe. The proper equipment helps prevent injuries and makes skating more enjoyable.

The main piece of equipment for skaters is the skateboard. A board is made of wood, usually maple, or plastic, depending on the style and quality of the board. A board, also called a **deck**, is commonly 31 inches (0.8 meters) long and 8 inches (0.2 m) wide. It has a textured cover for better grip. The deck is raised at both ends. The front is called a kicknose, and the back is called a kicktail.

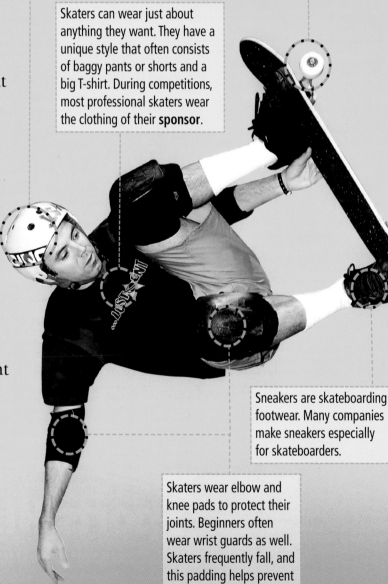

A helmet is one of the most important pieces of equipment a skater needs. Helmets prevent head injuries that can occur during a fall. It is especially important to wear a helmet when practicing or performing tricks.

There are four wheels attached to the bottom of the board. Wheels are often made of a strong plastic called polyurethane.

Skaters can wear just about anything they want. They have a unique style that often consists of baggy pants or shorts and a big T-shirt. During competitions, most professional skaters wear the clothing of their **sponsor**.

Sneakers are skateboarding footwear. Many companies make sneakers especially for skateboarders.

Skaters wear elbow and knee pads to protect their joints. Beginners often wear wrist guards as well. Skaters frequently fall, and this padding helps prevent them from getting hurt.

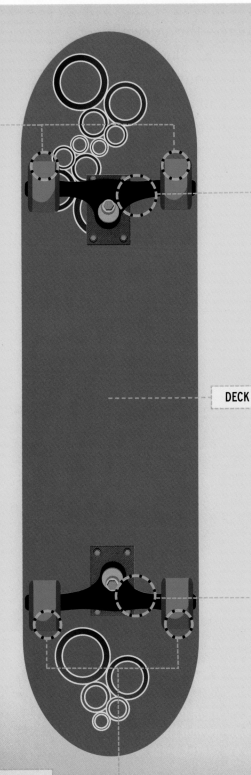

Trucks hold the wheels to the board using a base plate and a hanger. The base plate is screwed onto the board. The **axles** in the hanger hold the wheels. Trucks are made of light aluminum and allow a bit of movement between the hanger and base plate. This movement allows skaters to steer the board. The trucks are between 13 and 15 inches (0.3 and 0.4 meters) apart.

DECK TRUCK

☐ Like a skateboard, a scooter has a deck and wheels. Riders use their feet to push the scooter. Scooters also have a handlebar to help riders balance.

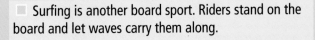

☐ Surfing is another board sport. Riders stand on the board and let waves carry them along.

☐ Early skateboards were simply pieces of wood with wheels attached.

WHEELS

Skateboarding can be done almost anywhere—the sidewalk, a gymnasium, an empty pool, or cement pond. Skateboarders want to stay safe and make sure the people around them are safe as well. They cannot practice tricks in a crowd of people. Skate parks across the country are great places for people to go just to skate. These parks have different ramps to suit all levels of skaters. Halfpipes are common ramps in skate parks. They are chutes with high, U-shaped walls. Skaters perform their tricks at the top of the ramps. Quarterpipes are similar to halfpipes but are one-sided.

Sports Venues

To find out more about skate parks from around the world, visit www.skateboardparks.com.

Skaters wait their turn to use a ramp.

Many different kinds of skateboarding are performed in different locations. Freestyle competitions are held on flat surfaces, and skaters perform tricks using just their boards and their imaginations. Street competitions use obstacles. Skaters have to use objects, such as railings and jumps, as they skate a course. Slalom competitors maneuver through a course of cones. Lastly, **vert** competitors use halfpipes or empty swimming pools. This is an extreme form of skateboarding.

Obstacles such as cones are jumped during street competitions.

Curved ramps were first built for skateboarders in Florida in 1975. The first skate park was opened in Port Orange, Florida in 1976.

The rule of skateboarding, for the most part, is that there are no set rules. In street competitions, skaters have to use the many different rails, quarterpipes, and boxes scattered throughout the course to show their skill.

For vert competitions, skaters coast the ramps showing their vertical tricks. Judges give points based on their impressions of the skater's performance. Judges also consider the variety and difficulty of the moves when awarding points. In this event, they look for new and creative uses of these obstacles as well as of the skateboard itself.

Some skaters compete in downhill races. They reach speeds of more than 35 miles per hour (56 kilometers per hour).

Tricks of the Trade

Skateboarding is an extreme sport. Some of the tricks athletes perform are very difficult.

Tricks

GRIND

HANDSTAND

KICKFLIP

NOSE STALL

In vert competitions, each skater has two runs of 45 seconds each to impress the judges with their best moves.

Style is important. Competitors need to make their tricks stand out from all the others. They also want to squeeze as many tricks into the time as possible. A new trick unfolds every 3 to 5 seconds. This keeps the crowd excited.

Judging skateboarding is a tough job because it is mostly based on the judges' opinions of the skater's ability. Most of the judges have competed in skateboarding. They know how difficult or original a trick is. If a skater performs original and challenging tricks, the judges will award them a high score out of 100.

Skateboarders must practice often to become good at many types of tricks.

Sports Science

Learn the science behind skateboarding at
www.exploratorium.edu/skateboarding.

Skateboarding can be a dangerous sport. Skaters spend most of their time in the air and can come down hard. To learn to skateboard, beginners also have to learn to fall. If a trick is not working, skaters **bail**. They kick the skateboard away from them while in the air. This way, they will not land on it when they fall.

Once the basics of skateboarding are mastered, tricks are the next step. The most basic trick on a ramp is a fakie. To do a fakie, skaters roll up a ramp wall forward and roll down it backward. Then, they roll up the other wall backward and roll down forward.

Not every town or city has a skate park, so many skaters skate wherever they can.

Only professional skateboarders should attempt tricks on large ramps.

Most skateboarding tricks are based on ollies. To do an ollie, skaters put one foot on the tail of the board and the other in the middle. They stomp down with their back foot and slide the other one up the board. They pull their knees up toward their chest and jump, bringing the board up with them. Then, they land on the board again. Skaters use this move to jump over obstacles.

Flips are popular skateboarding tricks. They are similar to ollies except skaters turn their boards over in the air. The kick flip is one of the easiest to learn. Skaters start out as if performing an ollie. Then, they push the back of their board toward the ground. When the tail hits the ground, they kick their front foot up and out to flip the board over.

The ollie is named for Allen Ollie Gelfand, who invented the move.

An ollie is any type of move where the skater jumps without hand-grabbing the board.

Kick turns are fun skateboarding tricks. Skaters lift their front wheels and turn 180 degrees or 360 degrees on the rear wheels. Then, the front of the board is returned to the ground. This trick can be done on flat ground and on ramps. There are many variations of this trick.

As a skater gets better and more confident, he or she can try more difficult tricks. Grinding is one of the toughest moves. Grinding is sliding along objects on one or both trucks. This trick can be done on steps, ramps, or rails. It is a true test of balance and skateboard control.

Grabbing the board with one hand is part of many tricks.

The faster the skater is going, the longer he or she will be able to grind an object.

Many skaters show their talent by spinning in the air. These tricks are called **airs**. Skaters rotate in mid-air in moves that are named after the degrees of their spin. A 360-degree spin is a full circle. Some skaters can complete 540-degree spins—such as the McTwist—or even 720-degree or 900-degree spins! Skaters face different directions and use different holds on their skateboards.

Skaters do not need ramps to perform tricks. Walls are fair game for many experienced skaters. A wallride is performed when athletes skate across a wall. Wallrides can be done facing the wall or away from the wall. To make the basic wallride more challenging and exciting, skaters can combine it with different moves.

Some skateboarders fly 10 feet (3 meters) off the ramp to perform a trick.

15

Many people begin skateboarding when they are young. They learn the basics of the sport and use it as a fun way to get around. As they get better, they start mastering more complicated tricks at skate parks or halfpipe ramps. To test their skills, many skaters enter competitions.

At the beginning, skaters need to win small, local competitions in order to **qualify** for regional competitions. Winning gives skaters access to national and international competitions. Once skaters have proven that they have what it takes to be champions, they can turn professional. Many professional skateboarders are sponsored by a skateboarding company or clothing manufacturer.

☐ Shaun White is a professional skateboarder and snowboarder who has won many awards for his skill.

Sports Events

Follow skateboarding events at http://espn.go.com/action/skateboarding/index.

There is no single skateboarding organization that puts together all the sport's tournaments. The International Association of Skateboard Companies and World Cup Skateboarding organize some of the well-known contests in the sport.

The most popular professional competition is the X Games. This event includes many other extreme sports, such as aggressive inline skating and BMX racing. Huge crowds watch athletes perform the best and toughest tricks at the X Games.

As a professional skateboarder, Andy Macdonald has won many gold medals in vert competitions.

The greatest skaters in the world gather at the X Games to battle for gold medals.

Superstars of Today

Skateboarding superstars make the sport even more exciting to watch.

Tony Hawk

BIRTH DATE: May 12, 1968
HOMETOWN: Carlsbad, California

CAREER FACTS:
- Tony began skateboarding as a teenager. He won his first professional competition in 1982. He went on to win 12 world titles.
- Tony has his own skateboard company called Birdhouse. He also sponsors a professional skateboarding team.
- Tony stars in a skateboarding video game. He also has his own clothing line.
- Tony is thought to be the greatest skateboarder ever. He can do two **consecutive** somersaults in mid-air and then land on his skateboard. He is also known as the first person to land a 900-degree spin in a vert competition.
- Tony retired from competition at 31 years old.

Andy Macdonald

BIRTH DATE: July 31, 1973
HOMETOWN: San Diego, California

CAREER FACTS:
- Andy became a professional skateboarder in 1994.
- Andy won the World Cup overall combined title Street and Vert from 1996 to 2000. In total, Andy has won the World Cup eight times.
- In August 1999, Andy introduced former president Bill Clinton at a press conference as part of the Partnership for a Drug-Free America campaign.
- Andy is a six-time X Games gold medalist in vert skating. He won the gold medal in the vert competition at the Gravity Games held in 2000.
- Andy appears in a skateboarding video game.
- Andy set the world distance record on a skateboard. He landed a jump of 52 feet 10 inches (16 meters).

Bob Burnquist

BIRTH DATE: October 10, 1976
HOMETOWN: Vista, California

CAREER FACTS:
- Bob was born in Rio de Janeiro, Brazil.
- Bob won the first professional competition he ever entered, in 1993.
- In competitions, Bob has to choose whether to skate street or vert. Skating both during one competition is too tiring.
- During the X Games in 1999 and 2006, Bob came in third for the best trick. Bob started the 2000 season by winning four of the first six competitions.
- In 2000, Bob won the vert title at the Globe Shoes World Cup.
- In 2007, Bob won gold at the X Games, in Big Air.
- In 2008, Bob also won gold in the X Games in the Mega Ramp competition and at the X Games in Brazil.

Elissa Steamer

BIRTH DATE: July 31, 1975
HOMETOWN: Fort Myers, Florida

CAREER FACTS:
- Elissa began skateboarding when she was only 12 years old.
- In 1998, Elissa became a professional skateboarder. She skates with the Toy Machine team.
- Elissa is the top female street skateboarder in the country. She was the first female skater to have her name on a professional skateboard.
- In 1998, she competed for the first time with other women skaters at the first All Girl Skate Jam.
- Elissa's moves can be seen in action sports videos and in Tony Hawk's ProSkater 2 video game.
- In 2004 and 2005, Elissa won gold in Street at the X Games.

Skateboarding can be hard on the body. Athletes need to work to stay strong and healthy. Eating a balanced diet is important. A diet with enough fruit and vegetables, breads and cereals, and milk and milk products helps keep athletes strong. It is also important for skateboarders to take in enough calories. Athletes use up more energy than people who do not exercise as much.

Drinking plenty of water before and after exercising is also very important. Athletes need to replace the water they lose through sweating.

■ Sports drinks help replace the energy you burn while skateboarding.

■ Skaters need to be fit and healthy to recover from the many cuts and bruises that result from falls. Dairy products and fruit provide some of the nutrients needed for a healthy diet.

No matter how many championships a skateboarder has won, he or she still needs to warm up before any physical activity. Stretching before skating helps prevent muscle strains and injuries. Skating uses leg, arm, and back muscles, so athletes need to make sure they stretch those areas before stepping onto their boards. After stretching, skaters start with simple moves to get their bodies warmed up and ready to skate.

■ Once skaters have warmed up, they can begin performing more challenging tricks.

■ Flexibility helps skaters maintain good balance and perform extreme tricks.

Skateboarding Brain Teasers

Test your skateboarding knowledge.
See if you can answers these questions!

Q What is the most popular professional skateboarding competition?

A The most popular professional competition is the X Games.

Q What are halfpipes?

A Halfpipes are common ramps in skate parks. They are chutes with high, U-shaped walls. Skaters perform their tricks at the top of the ramps.

Q How do skateboarders do a fakie?

A To do a fakie, skaters roll up a ramp wall forward and roll down it backward. Then, they roll up the other wall backward and roll down forward.

Q Who is the world's greatest skateboarder?

A Tony Hawk is thought to be the greatest skateboarder ever.

Q Who is the ollie named after?

A The ollie is named for Allen Ollie Gelfand, who invented the move.

Q Where was the first skate park?

A The first skate park was opened in Port Orange, Florida in 1976.

23

Glossary

airs: riding with all four wheels off the ground

axles: the bars or rods on which wheels turn

bail: falling, or dropping the skateboard in the middle of a trick

consecutive: in a row

deck: the flat-standing surface of a skateboard

qualify: earning the right to take part

sponsor: a person or company who offers funding for an athlete or team

trucks: the devices that hold skateboard wheels on the bottom of the board

vert: short for vertical, the use of ramps and other vertical structures designed for skating

Index